ALBERTINA MUSEUM, VIENNA

COVER: **YOUNG HARE**

ALBRECHT DÜRER'S PORTRAIT OF A HARE IS SO CAREFULLY PAINTED THAT ONE CAN COUNT THE HAIRS AROUND THE EYES AND NOSE.

DETAILS SUCH AS EARS, FUR, AND TOENAILS, LEND A MAGICAL REALISM TO THE PAINTING.

THE MORE ONE STUDIES THE EXPRESSION ON THE FACE THE MORE ONE FEELS THAT DÜRER'S **HARE** IS STUDYING THE VIEWER AS MUCH WITH ITS EARS AS WITH ITS EYES.

ALBRECHT DÜRER BELIEVED THAT THE PAINTER SHOULD HAVE A BROAD GENERAL EDUCATION TO RAISE HIM FROM CRAFTSMAN TO SCHOLAR.

HE WROTE: "THE ATTAINMENT OF TRUE, ARTISTIC, AND LOVELY EXECUTION IN PAINTING IS HARD TO COME UNTO: IT NEEDS A LONG TIME AND A HAND PRACTICED TO ALMOST PERFECT FREEDOM."

"GREAT MASTERSHIP...IS ONLY ATTAINED BY MUCH TOIL, LABOR, AND EXPENDITURE OF TIME."

"THAT MUST BE A STRANGELY DULL HEAD WHICH NEVER TRUSTS ITSELF TO FIND OUT ANYTHING FRESH BUT ONLY TRAVELS ALONG THE OLD PATH, SIMPLY FOLLOWING OTHERS AND NOT DARING TO REFLECT FOR ITSELF."

DÜRER WAS A GREAT PAINTER, WRITER, AND TEACHER.

PORTRAIT OF DÜRER BY RABOFF

DEDICATED TO FERNANDO PUMA

LIBRARY OF CONGRESS CATALOGING-IN-PUBLICATION DATA
RABOFF, ERNEST LLOYD.
    ALBRECHT DÜRER.
    (ART FOR CHILDREN)
REPRINT. ORIGINALLY PUBLISHED: GARDEN CITY, N.Y.: DOUBLEDAY, 1970. SUMMARY: A BRIEF BIOGRAPHY OF ALBRECHT DÜRER ACCOMPANIES FOURTEEN COLOR REPRODUCTIONS AND CRITICAL INTERPRETATIONS OF HIS WORKS. 1.DÜRER, ALBRECHT, 1471-1528 — CRITICISM AND INTERPRETATION — JUVENILE LITERATURE. 2. PAINTING, GERMAN—JUVENILE LITERATURE. 3. PAINTING, RENAISSANCE — GERMANY—JUVENILE LITERATURE. [1. DÜRER, ALBRECHT, 1471-1528. 2. ARTISTS. 3. PAINTING, GERMAN. 4. PAINTING, RENAISSANCE. 5. ART APPRECIATION] I. DÜRER, ALBRECHT, 1471-1528. II. TITLE. III. SERIES: ART FOR CHILDREN.
ND588.D9R17   1988   759.3   [92]   87-16863   ISBN 0-397-32216-X

ALBRECHT DÜRER

By Ernest Raboff

ART
FOR
CHILDREN

J. B. LIPPINCOTT · NEW YORK

ALBRECHT DÜRER WAS BORN ON MAY 21, 1471, IN NUREMBERG, GERMANY.

HIS FATHER WAS A GOLDSMITH AND HIS MOTHER WAS THE DAUGHTER OF A GOLDSMITH.

BY THE AGE OF 13, ALBRECHT, TRAINED BY HIS FATHER IN THE CRAFT OF MAKING BEAUTIFUL RINGS, CUPS, NECKLACES, AND OTHER FINE JEWELRY, DECIDED TO BECOME A PAINTER.

HE STUDIED FOR SEVERAL YEARS WITH A MASTER. THEN HE TRAVELED TO MANY CITIES AND FOREIGN COUNTRIES. HE MET AND LEARNED MUCH FROM STUDYING AND TALKING TO THE ARTISTS.

DÜRER WAS ONE OF THE FIRST ARTISTS TO RECORD HIS EXTENSIVE TRAVELS IN PAINTINGS AND IN LETTERS TO HIS FRIENDS.

HE BECAME FAMOUS FOR HIS OIL PAINTINGS, WATER COLORS, DRAWINGS, COPPER ENGRAVINGS, AND WOODCUTS.

DÜRER WAS A LIFE-LONG STUDENT AND LOVED KNOWLEDGE AS MUCH AS HE LOVED TO PAINT.

HE LIVED UNTIL 1528.

SELF PORTRAIT AT 13 YEARS

SELF PORTRAIT   THE LOUVRE, PARIS

"VIEW OF ARCO" IS A WATER COLOR PAINTING IN WHICH ALL THE LINES CURVE IN RHYTHM AND THE FORMS THEY CREATE RHYME LIKE A POEM.

A TOWN CLUSTERS AT THE BOTTOM OF THE INTERESTING MOUNTAIN. HIGH ABOVE IT IS A WALLED FORTRESS CITY.

DÜRER SEEMS TO HAVE PAINTED HIDDEN FACES THROUGH-OUT THIS RUGGED LANDSCAPE. YOU CAN FIND SOME BY LOOKING CAREFULLY AT THE DRAWING BELOW. PERHAPS YOU CAN FIND OTHERS IN THE PAINTING.

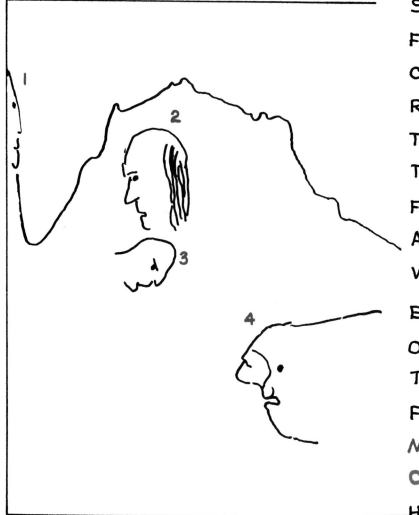

STARTING IN THE FOREGROUND, WE CAN STUDY THE ROCKY SLOPES, THE ROUND FULL TREES, THE PLANTED FIELDS, THE VILLAGE, AND THE STURDY WALLS.

EACH MOVEMENT OF OUR EYES TAKES US FARTHER UP THE MOUNTAIN TO THE CASTLE TOWER HIGH IN THE SKY.

VIEW OF ARCO   THE LOUVRE, PARIS

"THE HOUSE BY THE POND" IS A FINE WATER COLOR THAT INVITES US TO SIT ON THE EDGE OF THE POND AND ENJOY THE VIEW BEFORE US.

ALBRECHT DÜRER WAS A PATIENT MAN. EACH PIECE OF WOOD IN THE BOAT, EVERY BLADE OF GRASS, EACH CURVING BRANCH OF THE YOUNG TREES, EACH LINE OF THE HOUSE, AND STRAND OF CLOUD IS CAREFULLY AND TRUTHFULLY PAINTED.

DÜRER WAS ONE OF THE FIRST ARTISTS TO PAINT DIRECTLY FROM NATURE AND NOT JUST FROM MEMORY. AFTER MANY CENTURIES HE REMAINS ONE OF THE GREATEST REALISTS.

BY THOUGHTFUL STUDY OF HIS PAINTINGS AND WRITINGS WE CAN LEARN MUCH ABOUT THIS ARTIST'S LIFE AND HIS ENVIRONMENT.

AGNES DÜRER AND A GIRL FROM COLOGNE

THE HOUSE BY THE POND

"TWO MUSICIANS" WAS PAINTED ALMOST 500 YEARS AGO. IT WAS NOT UNTIL LATE IN THE 20TH CENTURY THAT SOME MEN, MANY OF THEM MUSICIANS, BEGAN TO WEAR THEIR HAIR LONG AND TO DRESS IN COLORFUL COSTUMES ONCE AGAIN.

ENTRANCE TO A QUARRY

DÜRER WAS A REPORTER OF HIS TIMES USING PICTURES TO TELL HIS STORIES.

WE KNOW WHAT DIFFERENT KINDS OF HATS, VESTS, SHAWLS, PANTS, AND SHOES WERE WORN.

WE CAN STUDY THE MUSICAL INSTRUMENTS THEY PLAYED.

THE HORN PLAYER WEARS THE SOOTHING COLORS OF WATER, AIR, AND GOLDEN EARTH WHILE THE OTHER ACCOM- PANIES HIM WITH BEATS OF HIS STICKS AGAINST THE DRUM.

TWO MUSICIANS   WALLRAF-RICHARTZ MUSEUM, COLOGNE

DÜRER'S "PEONIES" HAVE AN ALMOST HUMAN QUALITY.
IT IS AS THOUGH WALKING THROUGH A BRIGHT GARDEN
WE SUDDENLY CAME FACE TO FACE WITH A PEONY FAMILY.

ST. JEROME IN HIS STUDY   STATE MUSEUM, BERLIN (WEST)

THE ARTIST KNEW
THAT THERE ARE MALE
AND FEMALE PLANTS
IN NEARLY ALL OF
NATURE. MANY LOOK
QUITE DIFFERENT
FROM ONE ANOTHER.

HE KNEW THAT, AS
IS TRUE WITH BIRDS,
THERE CAN BE
DIFFERENCES IN
COLOR TOO.

PERHAPS DÜRER
PAINTED THE
TALLEST FLOWER WITH ITS DARKER GREEN LEAVES
TO BE THE MALE PEONY. BESIDE IT THE FEMALE BLOSSOM
WITH ITS BOWED PETALS IS PALER AND SOFTER.

THE YOUNG BUD, STRAIGHT AND SLENDER BEHIND
THEM, COMPLETES THE FAMILY CIRCLE.

PEONIES

ALBRECHT DÜRER'S "THE LITTLE OWL" SHOWS US A CALM, SMALL BIRD WITH EVERY FEATHER IN ITS PLACE.

HIS WINGS ARE FOLDED BACK. HIS LEGS STAND WITH THEIR LONG, SHARP, CURVING CLAWS FIRMLY BALANCING HIS ROUND BODY.

DÜRER'S WIFE, AGNES   ALBERTINA, VIENNA

THE OWL HAS BEEN A SYMBOL OF WISDOM FOR THOUSANDS OF YEARS. WE STILL USE THE EXPRESSION, "WISE AS AN OWL."

DÜRER KNEW THAT WE GATHER KNOWLEDGE WITH OUR EYES.

STUDY HIS OWL'S EYES.

1508

THE LITTLE OWL   ALBERTINA MUSEUM, VIENNA

"DÜRER'S FATHER" IS THE FIRST PORTRAIT AND THE LARGEST PAINTING IN OILS THIS ARTIST EVER CREATED. IT IS MORE THAN 48 BY 36 INCHES IN SIZE.

THE FATHER, IN ADDITION TO BEING A SCHOLAR AND ONE OF THE FINEST CRAFTSMEN OF HIS DAY, WAS THE DEVOTED PARENT OF 18 CHILDREN. ALBRECHT, HIS NAMESAKE, WAS HIS THIRD SON.

THE ARTIST SHOWS HIS FATHER AS A STRONG BUT GENTLE MAN. PERHAPS WE CAN SEE ON HIS FACE THE CARES OF PROVIDING SECURITY AND EDUCATION FOR SO LARGE A FAMILY. WE ALSO KNOW BY HIS FEATURES THAT HE WAS KIND AND THOUGHTFUL.

DÜRER DIRECTS OUR ATTENTION BY HIS USE OF COLOR AND CONTRAST TO HIS FATHER'S FACE AND CREATIVE HANDS. THE CLOTHES ARE SIMPLE. THEY SHOW US THAT THIS MAN HELD TALENT, HARD WORK, AND KNOWLEDGE IN HIGHER REGARD THAN MATERIAL POSSESSIONS.

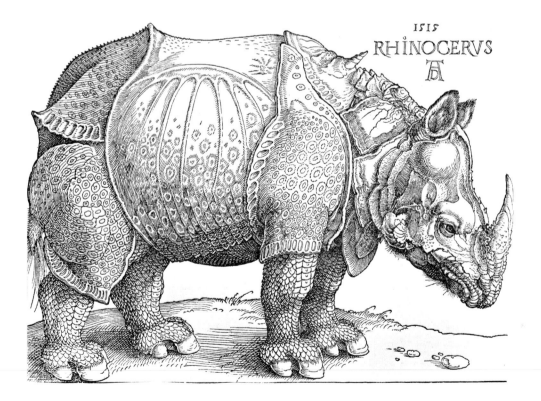

1515
RHINOCERVS

DÜRER'S FATHER   UFFICI GALLERY, FLORENCE

THE LARGE HORSE · STATE MUSEUM, BERLIN (WEST)

"THREE LINDEN TREES"
IS A STRONG REMINDER
THAT ALBRECHT DÜRER
RESPECTED AND ADMIRED
ALL FORMS OF LIFE.

HE PAINTED HIS TREES
SO THAT WE ARE AWARE OF
THEIR DIGNIFIED POSTURE,
THEIR GREAT STRENGTH OF
FORM, AND NOBLE HEADS.

THE SLENDER TREE TRUNKS
FIRMLY SUPPORT THEIR
HEAVY LOAD. THE BRANCHES,
BRIMMING WITH DARK GREEN
FOLIAGE, CREATE A PAINTING
IN A SINGLE COLOR.

IT IS A SONG OF GREEN IN AN ARRAY OF HUES.

WE KNOW BY THE SHADOWS UNDER THE TREES THAT IT IS
ALMOST NOON.
THE THICK
BLANKETS OF
GREEN SHADE
PROTECT THE
WATER-FILLED
ROOTS
FROM THE
OVERHEAD
SUN.

PORTRAIT DE GASPAR STURM · GIRAUDON, CHANTILLY, CONDE

THREE LINDEN TREES   KUNSTHALLE, BREMEN

EUSTACE STATE MUSEUM, BERLIN (WEST)

"THE VILLAGE OF KALCHREUTH" RESEMBLES A MODERN SUMMER RESORT.

THE ART OF ARCHITECTURE, LIKE PAINTING, MUSIC, AND LITERATURE, IS TIMELESS.

IN DÜRER'S VILLAGE, STEEP ROOFED HOUSES AND BARNS CLUSTER PROTECTIVELY TOGETHER BEYOND THE WHEEL-RUTTED ROAD.

MASSIVE SHADE TREES, DISTANT ORCHARDS, THE ROLLING PASTURE LANDS, AND THE SURROUNDING LOW HILLS HOLD THE COMMUNITY LIKE A WHITE BALL IN THE POCKET OF A GREEN GLOVE.

THE CHARM, THE QUIET PEACE, THE UNHURRIED CONVERSA-TION OF THE COUPLE AT REST UNDER THE TREE, THE CLEAR AIR, AND BRIGHT SUNLIGHT HAVE GREAT APPEAL FOR OUR EYES AS WELL AS FOR OUR MINDS.

1518

1507

kalt und . DA

VILLAGE OF KALCHREUTH   KUNSTHALLE, BREMEN

ALBRECHT DÜRER'S "COLUMBINE"
SPLASHES BEFORE OUR EYES LIKE A
DELICATE WATER FOUNTAIN.

THIN JETS OF GREEN AND RED STEMS AND LONG GRACE-
FULLY CURVING STREAMLETS OF GRASS CREATE A BLUE-
GREEN VEIL OF INTERWOVEN LINES. THE COLUMBINE LEAVES
SEEM TO FLOAT ACROSS THIS PATTERN LIKE HOVERING

THE WALK   STATE MUSEUM, BERLIN (WEST)

DRAGONFLIES
AND
BUTTERFLIES.

OR
WE CAN IMAGINE
THAT WE ARE SEEING
A MOSS COVERED
EASTER BONNET
SPIRED WITH
LIVING GRASS
AND
BLOOMING COLUMBINE.

A GREAT WORK OF
ART HAS THE MAGIC
TO CARRY US FROM
THE REALITY OF
THE ARTIST'S VISION
INTO
THE WONDERLANDS
OF OUR MINDS.

COLUMBINE   ALBERTINA MUSEUM, VIENNA

"INNSBRUCK AND THE PATSCHERKOFEL" IS A BEAUTIFUL EXAMPLE OF DÜRER'S GENIUS AT COMBINING THE VISUAL CRAFT OF THE REPORTER AND THE POETIC COLOR OF THE SENSITIVE ARTIST.

THE ENTIRE PAINTING SHIMMERS WITH THE GLOWING HIGHLIGHTS AND REFLECTIONS OF A FAIRYTALE SCENE.

EVERY DETAIL IS FAITHFULLY RECORDED. WE HAVE A FEELING OF REALITY YET WE ARE CAUGHT IN THE MAKE-BE-LIEVE ENCHANTMENT OF THIS WATER COLOR.

EACH WINDOW, EACH EAVE, SPIRE, TURRET, WALL, DOORWAY, RIPPLE OF WATER, AND BILLOW OF CLOUD HAS ITS OWN SHAPE AND PERSONALITY.

MUSE THALIA

DÜRER MODELED EVERYTHING HE ENGRAVED, DREW, OR PAINTED WITH AN INTENSE LOVE FOR TRUTH AND WITH A MASTERY OF THE TOOLS OF HIS CRAFT. HE PROFOUNDLY BELIEVED THAT EVERYTHING MAN SEES POSSESSES LIFE.

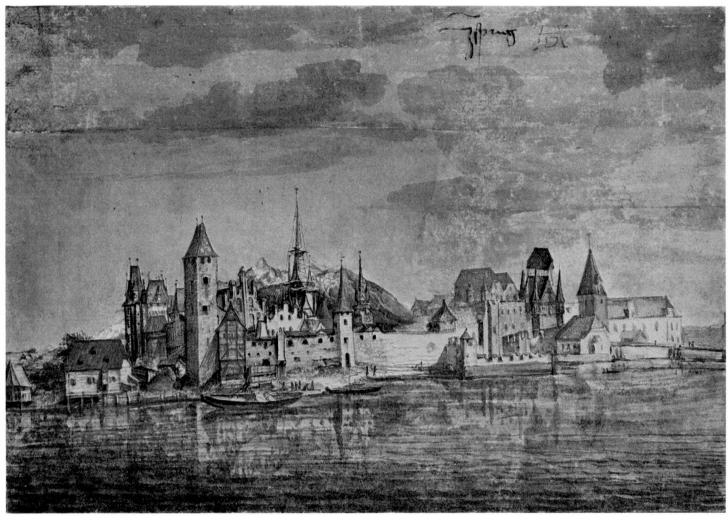

INNSBRUCK AND THE PATSCHERKOFEL   ALBERTINA MUSEUM, VIENNA

AGNES DÜRER   KUNSTHALLE, BREMEN

"THE LARGE PIECE OF TURF"
IS LIKE A SYMPHONY
PLAYED ON BLADES OF GRASS
AND STALKS OF REEDS.

PAINTERS SUCH AS DÜRER
ARE COMPOSERS OF VISUAL
MUSIC WHERE LINE, FORM,
AND COLOR CAN BE CHANGED
INTO SIGHT-SOUNDS EVEN
AS MUSIC CREATES MENTAL
PICTURES.

IN OUR IMAGINATION BROAD LEAVES SEEM LIKE DRUMS; SMALL
LEAVES MAY BE LIKE TRUMPETS AND SLENDER HORNS.
THICK REED STALKS COULD BE CELLOS. THIN REEDS
REMIND US OF FINE VIOLINS WHILE THE GRASSES SEEM
TO WEAVE HARMONIES LIKE CLARINETS AND FLUTES.

IT IS FUN TO USE OUR EYES LIKE EARS. ALSO, IT HELPS
US BETTER TO UNDERSTAND AND APPRECIATE THE
FINE ART OF PAINTING.

THE VISITATION   STATE MUSEUM, BERLIN (WEST)

CHRIST APPEARS TO MARY   STATE MUSEUM, BERLIN (WEST)

THE LARGE PIECE OF TURF   ALBERTINA MUSEUM, VIENNA

THIS "SELF-PORTRAIT" WAS PAINTED BY DÜRER WHEN HE WAS 29 YEARS OLD.

IT IS DESIGNED SO THAT BOTH THE FACE AND THE RIGHT HAND, ESPECIALLY THE EYES AND THE FINGERS HE USED TO GRASP THE PAINT BRUSHES, RECEIVE OUR ATTENTION FIRST.

FOR A PAINTER TO BECOME AN ARTIST, FOR ANY CRAFTSMAN OR PROFESSIONAL TO BECOME A TRULY CREATIVE PERSON, THAT INDIVIDUAL MUST BE A SCIENTIST, AN OBJECTIVE OBSERVER, A NATURALIST AND HUMANIST.

DÜRER WROTE: "LOVE AND DELIGHT..ARE BETTER TEACHERS OF THE ART OF PAINTING THAN COMPULSION IS...

"I WOULD GLADLY GIVE EVERYTHING I KNOW FOR THE GOOD OF STUDENTS WHO PRIZE ART MORE HIGHLY THAN SILVER OR GOLD."

HANDS OF AN APOSTLE

1500

AD

Albertus Durerus Noricus
ipsum me propriis sic essin
gebam coloribus aetatis
anno XXVIII.

SELF PORTRAIT   ALTE PINAKOTHEK MUSEUM, MUNICH